CRAIGSLIST

DISCARD

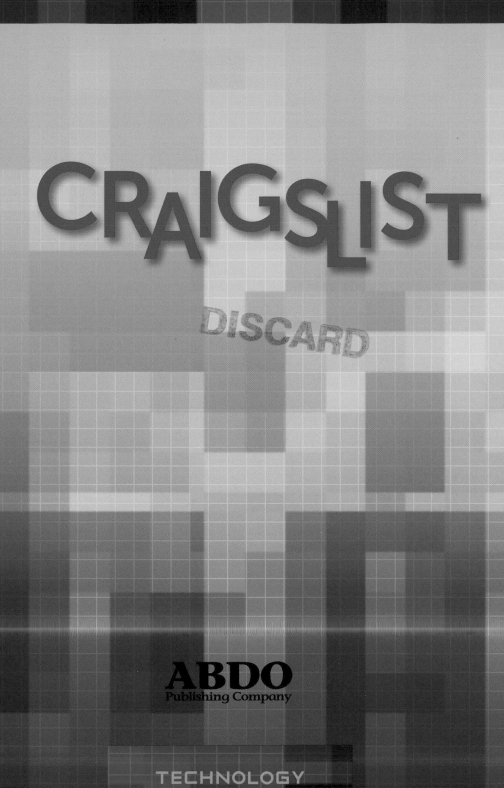

ABDO
Publishing Company

TECHNOLOGY
PIONEERS

CRAIGSLIST

THE COMPANY AND ITS FOUNDER

by Susan M. Freese

Content Consultant
Charles Steinfeld,
Professor and Chair, Department of Telecommunication,
Information Studies, and Media
Michigan State University

CREDITS

Published by ABDO Publishing Company, 8000 West 78th Street, Edina, Minnesota 55439. Copyright © 2011 by Abdo Consulting Group, Inc. International copyrights reserved in all countries. No part of this book may be reproduced in any form without written permission from the publisher. The Essential Library™ is a trademark and logo of ABDO Publishing Company.

Printed in the United States of America,
North Mankato, Minnesota
112010
012011

Editor: Rebecca Rowell
Copy Editor: David Johnstone
Interior Design and Production: Craig Hinton
Cover Design: Emily Love

Library of Congress Cataloging-in-Publication Data
Freese, Susan M., 1958-
  Craigslist : the company and its founder / by Susan M. Freese.
      p. cm. -- (Technology pioneers)
  Includes bibliographical references and index.
  ISBN 978-1-61714-806-4
  1. Craigslist.com (Firm)--History--Juvenile literature. 2. Internet advertising--Juvenile literature. 3. Internet marketing--Juvenile literature. 4. Online social networks--Juvenile literature. 5. Newmark, Craig. 6. Businessmen--United States--Biography. I. Title.
  HF6146.I58F74 2011
  381'.14206573--dc22
                                        2010042448

TABLE OF CONTENTS

Craig Newmark, founder of Craigslist, is also part of its customer service team.

A UNIQUE COMPANY FOUNDER

Anyone who has held a position in the customer service department of a store or other business will say the job is thankless. Mostly, it involves listening to customers' criticisms and complaints and trying to find acceptable solutions. People rarely, if ever, contact customer service to say thanks or good job, and they are not always happy with the solutions provided.

So, it is highly unusual that Craig Newmark, founder and chairperson of Craigslist, decided to work in the customer service area of his company. Craigslist is an online network of classified advertisements and discussion groups. People go to this Web site to buy and sell items and services and to share information and opinions. Users can also meet people via the site. An estimated 50 million Americans use Craigslist each month, which means providing customer service is a huge job.

As part of Craigslist's customer service team, Newmark spends approximately 50 hours per week responding to customers' e-mails. In one year, he receives almost 200,000 e-mails and sends out roughly 40,000 responses. Most days, he starts reviewing e-mails on his computer at home even before he has breakfast or takes a shower.

Newmark believes Craigslist's amazing success is due mainly to providing high-quality service. It is not surprising, then, that Newmark

"It's just a simple platform where people help each other out with everyday stuff, like getting a job or a place to live. Beyond that, somehow we have created a community. There are issues, but we do trust people."[1]

—*Craig Newmark*

calls himself a "customer service rep and founder at Craigslist."[2] Customer service comes first—always. Newmark's focus on service, not profits, is one of several factors that make him a unique company founder.

THE GOLDEN RULE

The idea of people treating others as they would like to be treated is commonly referred to as the Golden Rule. Perhaps the most common statement of this rule is from the book of Luke (6.31) in the New Testament: "Do to others as you would have them do to you."[3] Many other religions share this belief in what is called ethical reciprocity, or the fair and equal treatment of all people. Statements of this belief can be found in the writings of the Buddhist, Hindu, Islamic, Jewish, and Confucian religions, as well as the spiritual traditions of many Native American peoples.

GETTING OUT OF THE WAY

In the early days of Craigslist, Newmark gained some important insights about his own abilities. For instance, Newmark recognized he was not an effective manager. Although he had a successful career as a computer programmer, he was not good at running a business. Realizing he needed help, Newmark brought in Jim Buckmaster to manage and expand the company's operations. Buckmaster proved himself quickly. Within a year, Newmark made him the company's president and chief executive officer (CEO).

Making Buckmaster the president and CEO was an unusual

Jim Buckmaster became the CEO and president of Craigslist in 2000.

move. Few heads of companies—especially new, fast-growing companies—would be willing to give up that control. But Newmark knew he needed to step aside and let someone else take over. In his words, "Sometimes the best thing you can do is get out of the way."[4]

GIVING PEOPLE A BREAK

Soon after starting Craigslist, Newmark also determined that he was good at providing customer service. Looking back, he said,

From the very beginning, I was involved in talking to people; listening to people. And it hasn't stopped. The idea was that people send me information; I'd ask them about it, listen, try to do something about it— and then ask for more feedback.[5]

In customer service, Newmark handles a lot of complaints about advertisements that violate Craigslist's guidelines. The site's

REVOLUTIONARY WORDS

Some sources have said Newmark's belief in knowing when to get out of the way is based on a famous saying from the 1960s—an era of social and political unrest. Newmark was a teenager during most of that era, in which many Americans protested against the Vietnam War (1954–1975), racial discrimination, and widespread poverty. The saying "Lead, follow, or get out of the way" was used to encourage people to work for change or to stand aside and let others do it.

Other sources, however, have traced the saying to Thomas Paine, a supporter of the American Revolution (1775–1783). Born in England, Paine emigrated from his homeland to the British colonies in North America in 1774, where he settled in Philadelphia. He began a career as a journalist and soon became well known for his revolutionary ideas.

The saying "Lead, follow, or get out of the way" does not appear in either *Common Sense* or *The Crisis*, Paine's best-known works. Scholars have concluded that Payne wrote it in one of his letters. In all his writing, Paine used plain language and clear logic to try to convince people of the colonies' need to become independent.

users are expected to follow certain rules about the number and kinds of ads allowed. People who break these rules will likely have their ads removed by Newmark or his customer service team.

In one case, however, Newmark made an exception. He decided to help a photographer who had posted more ads for his services than allowed by Craigslist guidelines. The photographer seemed desperate for work, Newmark thought. So, rather than delete the ads, Newmark asked the photographer to place them in specific categories on Craigslist, such as Special Events. The photographer agreed to that solution. According to Newmark, reasoning with people almost always works.

Newmark has sympathy for people who are looking for work, and he believes that trying to help someone find a job is honorable. He also believes that people should treat others as they want to be treated. These beliefs are reflected in Craigslist's company motto: "Give people a break."[6]

DEALING WITH TRAGEDY

Some of the ads posted on Craigslist have drawn people into dangerous situations and made them victims of crimes. Newmark takes these cases

TRACING E-MAILS AND WEB POSTINGS

When someone sends an e-mail or posts information online, his or her computer leaves a trail. Following this trail will provide information about the message, including its subject, the date it was created, the date it was received, who sent it, and who received it. Tracing a message or posting from a home or work computer is fairly easy. Tracing a message or posting from a computer at a library or an Internet café, which has many users, is more difficult—and sometimes impossible.

personally, so they receive his immediate and direct attention.

In one case, Newmark worked with the police to track down someone who had stolen a woman's laptop at gunpoint. The robber later sold the computer after advertising it on Craigslist, police believed. When phone calls to the seller went unanswered, the police contacted Newmark. He helped them identify the seller through the e-mail address used to post the Craigslist ad.

In a few tragic cases, people responding to Craigslist ads have been murdered. In the first case, a 24-year-old woman was killed when she went to a suburban Minneapolis, Minnesota, home expecting to be interviewed for a babysitting job—a job advertised on Craigslist.

The day after the woman's family learned of her death, they received a short handwritten note from Newmark via Federal Express. In it, he stated his condolences and then added, "Please contact me if you want to talk further. Here's my e-mail, here's my phone number, I'm available anytime."[7] After the woman's funeral, her father e-mailed Newmark, thanking him for the note. Newmark responded immediately, saying, "If there is anything we can do to support your efforts, don't hesitate to contact me."[8] After more than a year of correspondence, Newmark and Buckmaster agreed to have Craigslist sponsor a memorial concert for the young woman.

The woman's family was impressed by Craigslist's willingness to be involved in the memorial. One family member commented:

> *They didn't hesitate. And I think a company, sometimes they would be leery about putting their names on the line. But they were up front right away to say, "Nope. This is important to us. This is an important statement." And that was surprising to us.[9]*

Not everyone has approved of how Craigslist has responded to such tragedies. Members of law enforcement and the media have claimed that Craigslist has not done enough to prevent more crimes from occurring. Some critics have suggested that Craigslist is partly responsible for the crimes,

"You do customer service for 14 years or so, and that changes you. You interact with thousands of people, you see, if you're really paying attention, that you'll have to handle a lot of negative situations."[10]

—*Craig Newmark*

and several law enforcement agencies have filed criminal charges against the company. More and more, Craig Newmark has found himself having to defend the company that bears his name. +

Katherine Ann Olson was killed after answering a Craigslist ad in Minnesota.

Craig became interested in computers when he was in college.

LIFE BEFORE CRAIGSLIST

Craig Alexander Newmark was born on December 5, 1952, in Morristown, New Jersey. His mother, Joyce, was a bookkeeper. His father, Lee, was a traveling salesman who sold products ranging from meat to insurance. The two, both Jewish, met at a synagogue dance and were married three years later.

Craig was raised Jewish and celebrated his bar mitzvah when he was 13. Although Craig would not continue to practice the Jewish religion later in life, he would hold onto the values he was taught as a child. Looking back, he said,

> *I'm finding the values I learned as a kid are the values that work for me but they are the same values that pretty much everyone in the world is taught. The idea's to practice what one preaches.*[1]

Craig's father died of lung cancer in 1966, just six months after Craig's bar mitzvah. His mother continued to work and to raise Craig and a younger son, Jeff. When Craig was asked about growing up in a single-parent

MORRISTOWN, NEW JERSEY

Morristown, Craig's hometown, is in northern New Jersey, between New York City and Philadelphia, Pennsylvania. Because of this key location, Morristown was selected by General George Washington and the Continental Army as the site of several winter encampments during the Revolutionary War. The area of their encampments has been preserved as a National Historic Park.

home, he said, "We weren't poor, but not incredibly far from there."[2]

SCHOOL DAYS

As a child, Craig was a good student and thought about becoming some kind of scientist. An early interest in dinosaurs made him want to be a paleontologist, who studies prehistoric life. Later, Craig thought about becoming a theoretical physicist, who uses high-level math and science to explain natural events. He was drawn to this field because at that time, the early 1960s, Americans were becoming fascinated by nuclear power.

In high school, Craig was cocaptain of the debate team. He was also a member of the forensics club, a group of students interested in debate and public speaking. With several friends, he started a club for playing Go, a challenging strategic board game popular in Asia.

Throughout his youth, Craig was a loner. While he was a member of some school clubs, he was rarely invited to parties or included in other social events. In high school, a worried teacher sent him to the guidance counselor's office for therapy. The counselor ended up teaching him how to play chess.

One of Craig's earliest interests was dinosaurs, so he thought about becoming a paleontologist.

When Craig reflects on his childhood, he describes himself as a nerd and says he had some problems getting along with other kids. He admits to having worn a plastic pocket protector and thick glasses that were sometimes held together by tape—both traits often associated with being a nerd.

Perhaps because he spent a lot of time by himself, Craig developed a love of reading. He especially enjoyed reading science fiction and comic books.

Craig graduated from Morristown High School in 1971. His hard work and success as a student earned him several college scholarships. Having these funds was essential to continuing his education, given his family's financial struggles.

COLLEGE LIFE

Craig attended Case Western Reserve University in Cleveland, Ohio. This private research university was well known for its science and engineering programs. At first, Craig planned to study physics, but he became interested in computers, which were then a new technology. He realized this field offered many possibilities

ON BEING A NERD

"I'm still a nerd at heart, but in ways I think are good, in that when you grow up as a nerd, you do remember what it feels like a little to be left out. In turning that around, it reminds you that the Internet includes, or potentially includes, everyone."[3]

—*Craig Newmark*

for future employment. Working with his professors, he designed his own program of study in computer science.

Craig continued to be a loner, finding it difficult to make friends and enjoy college life. Then, he had a revelation. In his second year of college, he read a book about the different types and uses of language. Upon reading the book, Craig realized, "It wasn't everyone else who had a communication problem. It had to be me. I miss what other people would find obvious."[4]

Despite making this self-discovery, Craig remained isolated throughout college. He focused on his studies and spent more and more time alone, working with computers. Looking back, he said, "I was academically smart, emotionally stupid. I can't read people, and I take them too literally."[5]

CASE WESTERN RESERVE UNIVERSITY

Case Western Reserve University was formed in 1967, just four years before Newmark enrolled there. It was created by the merger of two long-established colleges in Cleveland, Ohio: the Case Institute of Technology, founded in 1881, and Western Reserve University, founded in 1826. The two schools had been sharing faculty and buildings for decades, so merging seemed an obvious decision. The schools' leaders realized that merging would form a nationally recognized university. The Case Institute was well known for its science and engineering programs, and Western Reserve University was well known for its liberal arts and professional programs.

During his six years at Case Western, Craig earned a bachelor of science in 1975 and a master of science in 1977. Both degrees were in computer science. Once again, his academic success was rewarded. Even before he graduated, computer giant IBM offered him a job.

STARTING A CAREER

Newmark's first job at IBM took him to Boca Raton, Florida, where he worked as a computer programmer in the company's development lab. Getting a position in this lab, which involved creating new computer technology, was quite

INVENTION OF THE PERSONAL COMPUTER

The personal computer (PC) was designed as a stand-alone machine to be used by a single person. Its small size and reduced price were made possible by the invention of the microchip. A microchip is a miniature unit of electronic circuits that can perform many functions. The first microchips could perform about 10 functions; today, microchips can perform billions of functions at once.

PCs were first available to the public in the late 1970s. Most were built from kits by computer hobbyists. One of the first models available for sale was the Apple II, which was introduced by Apple Computer in 1977. Radio Shack and Commodore also released PCs that year. IBM entered the market in 1981 and quickly dominated sales. Other manufacturers soon copied the IBM PC, creating so-called clones. By the end of the 1980s, technological developments had made it possible for many individuals to own and use PCs.

The PC was one of the most important inventions of the twentieth century. *Time* magazine recognized this as early as 1982, when it named the PC its Machine of the Year. This was the first time the magazine had given this honor to something other than a person.

an achievement for a young college graduate. At the time, the late 1970s, the use of personal computers was new. Huge mainframe computers that occupied entire rooms were being used in business and industry.

After six years in Florida, Newmark worked at IBM for ten years in Detroit, Michigan, and then for one year in Pittsburgh, Pennsylvania. He climbed the career ladder at the company, moving from computer programming into sales. He hoped being a salesperson would help him improve his social skills.

Meeting people and making friends did not come naturally to Newmark, however. He looked for ways to develop his personal life. Taking classes seemed to provide a good way to meet people, so he took a photography course. To try to meet women, in particular, he also took courses in yoga and ballet. Newmark had never been athletic, though, and ended up getting hurt. After several injuries, he gave up these activities.

In 1993, after working for IBM for 17 years, Newmark quit. Years later, he admitted that he should have quit sooner. Friends said he was mistreated by his managers, but Newmark does not agree. In his words, "Some of them were trying to help me, and I didn't get it. . . . I had difficulties dealing with people."[6]

Eager for something new, the 40-year-old Newmark went to work for Charles Schwab, a large investment bank, in San Francisco, California. Although he did not realize it at the time, this move would change his life in several unbelievable ways. +

In 1970, IBM computers were the size of an entire room!

Newmark moved to San Francisco in 1993.

STARTING CRAIGSLIST

Upon arriving in San Francisco, Newmark immediately felt at home. Years later, he said, "I've been a San Franciscan all my life, although I only moved here in mid '93."[1] At the time, San Francisco's unique population and culture also appealed to Newmark. Located on the northern edge of Silicon Valley, a rapidly growing center of technology, the city was attracting many well-educated and highly intelligent individuals. They enjoyed music, art, theater, and other cultural events.

In addition, these individuals believed their work was important in bringing about not only technological progress but also social change. Use of technology on a personal level took off in the 1990s. More and more people across the United States owned personal computers and accessed the Internet. It was an exciting time to work in the high-tech industry.

CREATING A NETWORK OF FRIENDS AND COWORKERS

Much of Newmark's job at Charles Schwab involved analyzing computer security. That included

SILICON VALLEY

Silicon Valley, located 45 miles (72 km) southeast of San Francisco, is considered the technology center of the United States. Creating this center was the idea of Frederick Terman, a professor of electrical engineering at Stanford University. Stanford is located in Palo Alto, in the middle of the valley. Beginning in 1954, Terman encouraged his students to start their own companies in the Stanford Industrial Park. Among those students were William Hewlett and David Packard, who formed the company Hewlett-Packard. The name *silicon* refers to the many companies in the area that have, over the years, produced cutting-edge technology using silicon chips, which drive computers.

observing people's use of the Internet. Newmark saw a lot of people using this new technology to help others, and he thought he should do the same thing.

In early 1995, Newmark started e-mailing friends and coworkers about interesting arts and technology events in San Francisco. People started asking for other kinds of information, such as leads on apartments and jobs. As Newmark's e-mail list grew, he encouraged people to add their own information to it. By mid-1995, his list grew to more than 200 names. Contacting this many individuals using e-mail became challenging, so Newmark created a listserv, which is a database of e-mail addresses. Using the listserv, which he named Craigslist, allowed Newmark to contact everyone with a single e-mail.

In 1995, Newmark quit his job at Charles Schwab and began working as a computer consultant. This meant he was self-employed, rather than working for a company as one of its employees. During the next four years, he completed projects for many companies, including General Motors, Bank of America, and Sun Microsystems. Newmark discovered he preferred working on his own to being employed by a big company. "I had more fun, more challenge, more time off and, frankly, software

While working for Charles Schwab, Newmark began e-mailing a list of San Francisco events to his friends and coworkers.

contracting was more lucrative than what I was doing," he later noted.[2]

While Newmark pursued his career as a consultant in 1995, he continued to work on Craigslist. The number of recipients had quickly grown too large to accommodate using a listserv. So Newmark put his computer programming skills to use and created a Web site. There, anyone could access the ads, not only his e-mail recipients.

The new Web site needed a name. Newmark wanted to name it after San Francisco and considered calling it SF Events or something similar. But, as he recalled, "People who were smarter than me said, 'Hey, we already call it Craigslist. Let's keep it personal and quirky and just call it Craigslist.'"[3]

EARLY MILESTONES

By the end of 1997, three milestones had occurred in the growth of the Web site that made Newmark realize Craigslist was something unique. The first milestone occurred when Craigslist had 1 million page views. The site was being visited 1 million times per month, although not necessarily by 1 million different people. Craigslist had rapidly become one of the most popular English-language Web sites in the world.

The second milestone came when Newmark was asked to run banner ads on Craigslist. Banner ads are paid advertisements that run on Web pages. The request came from Microsoft Sidewalk, a division of the giant software company. Newmark declined the request for two reasons: he did not want to clutter the site with ads, and he did not want to make the site a profit-earning business.

The third milestone in Craigslist's early development occurred when people offered to help Newmark run the Web site on a volunteer basis.

People were committed to the site and to serving the Internet community. Newmark tried to run the site with volunteers for about a year but felt it did not work. He later admitted that the failure was due mostly to his own lack of leadership.

In 1998, some friends helped Newmark get "out of denial about what was going on."[4] Clearly, Craigslist was on the verge of incredible success. Early the following year, Newmark ended his consulting work and focused full-time on Craigslist. He also set up the company as a corporation, which gave it a legal structure.

TWO VERY DIFFERENT LEADERS

Craig Newmark and Jim Buckmaster are quite different, particularly in appearance. Buckmaster is exactly one foot (30 cm) taller than Newmark. In addition, Buckmaster has dark, wavy hair and is quite thin, in contrast to Newmark, who is bald and a bit overweight.

In terms of personality, Newmark has been described as goofy and chatty, whereas Buckmaster has been called shy and shrewd. Buckmaster admits to having been somewhat carefree and unfocused as a young adult. Newmark was much more determined to further his education and career. In the early days of developing Craigslist, the two disagreed about using a purple peace sign as a logo or icon throughout the Web site. Newmark did not want to use the peace sign, but Buckmaster put it on the site anyway. Newmark eventually came to accept it.

Perhaps because of their differences, Newmark and Buckmaster make good partners. As one interviewer wrote,

Buckmaster would never have invented Craigslist. But—picture Henry Ford [who invented the automobile] redesigned by Ralph Nader [a consumer advocate]—it was he who took the simple machine Newmark had invented and put it on the road for everyone.[5]

HIRING JIM BUCKMASTER

Within months of working full-time at Craigslist, Newmark realized he was not good at running a company. He was not tough enough in business dealings, and he had made several bad decisions in hiring people.

Newmark made a key decision in 1999, when he hired Jim Buckmaster as a computer programmer and Web developer. Newmark did so after he found Buckmaster's résumé posted on Craigslist. Buckmaster took the job instead of one that paid more, because he recognized that Craigslist was a unique company.

When Buckmaster went to work for Craigslist, the Web site had many limitations. One was that the site included ads of interest only to people in San Francisco. Furthermore, every ad had to be reviewed, approved, and posted manually by a Craigslist employee. Finally, the Web site did not have a

WHAT IS A CORPORATION?

A corporation is a type of company. It is a legal structure formed by one or more owners. Owners purchase or are given shares of stock, depending on how much of the company they own. A corporation can enter into contracts to do business, hire and fire employees, borrow money and take on debt, pay taxes, and many other things. The corporation, not its owners, is responsible for its contracts, debts, and decisions. Many business owners form a corporation in order to have this protection, which is called limited liability.

search engine, which users could use to look through the many postings more quickly and more easily than searching the site page by page.

All of these things changed under Buckmaster's direction. In June 2000, Craigslist was launched in Boston, Massachusetts. Two months later, it was launched in several other major US cities: New York, Chicago, Los Angeles, Portland, Seattle, and Washington DC. Each of these metropolitan areas had its own site that included information specific to the area. In 2001, Craigslist launched its first international site in Vancouver, British Columbia. The first site outside North America—in London—soon followed. In 2004, the Web site expanded to five cities in non–English speaking countries: Amsterdam, Bangalore, Paris, Saõ Paulo, and Tokyo.

Also under Buckmaster's guidance, a self-posting system was put in place that allowed users to post, review, and approve ads themselves. A flagging system was added, too, so users could point

DISCOVERING A CAREER

Buckmaster did not set out to be a computer programmer or Web developer. In his words, "I backed into computers as a way to make a living. Originally I was computer-phobic." A coworker at the University of Michigan introduced him to the World Wide Web. Buckmaster said, "It was a religious experience I was so absorbed that I didn't get out of my chair from 5 p.m. to 8 a.m. the next day."[6]

out potential problems with ads they found on the site, such as posts that did not seem legitimate. In addition, the categories of ads were expanded, and discussion boards were created for people to share political and legal views. Finally, a search engine was added to the site.

According to Newmark, Buckmaster was "a natural manager."[7] Only 11 months after hiring him, Newmark made Buckmaster the company's president and CEO. Newmark kept his position as chairperson of Craigslist's board of directors and continued to work in customer service. He has summed up his work relationship with Buckmaster by saying, "The deal is he makes things happen, leaving me the time to listen."[8] +

Newmark, *left*, and Buckmaster manage the growing business of Craigslist from their San Francisco office.

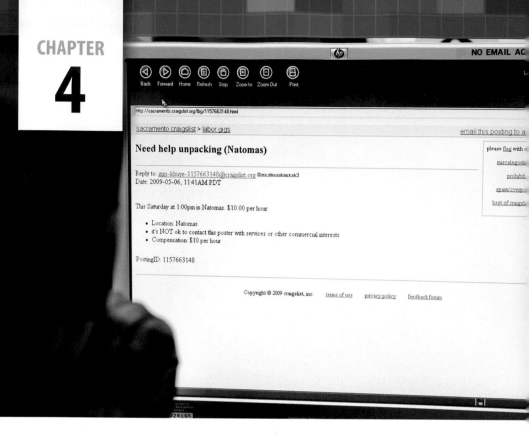

Craigslist has become a popular site to post and search for jobs.

AMAZING SUCCESS

With Newmark and Buckmaster working together, Craigslist grew quickly. By 2004, the Web site was available in more than 30 cities, most spanning the United States, with two in Canada and one in England. By 2009, it had spread to 700 cities in 70 countries. Worldwide, users were posting more than 50 million new classified ads each month, including 1 million job announcements. Another 120 million users were posting opinions in the site's discussion forums. In the United States, more than 50 million people use Craigslist every month—one in five adults.

A "HAPPY ACCIDENT"

Many in the business world consider Craigslist an amazing success story, but Newmark calls it a "happy accident."[1] The company has not followed a traditional business model or plan. "We just have a very odd business model," explains Newmark. "Our business model, in a sense, is we can do well in business by doing good for people."[2]

For instance, unlike most companies, Craigslist does not accept paid advertising. Newmark established this policy in the early days of the company, when he

MOST POPULAR WEB SITES

In August 2010, these were the ten most popular Web sites among Americans, based on monthly use:
1. Google.com
2. Facebook.com
3. Yahoo.com
4. YouTube.com
5. Amazon.com
6. Wikipedia.org
7. Twitter.com
8. Craigslist.org
9. eBay.com
10. Blogger.com

turned down Microsoft's request to run paid ads. At the time, he decided not to clutter the Web site with ads and not to make it a profit-earning business. Then and now, the company's primary means of promotion has been word of mouth.

Over the years, Newmark has also turned down countless investors and suggestions for making the Web site more profitable. According to one source, by refusing both advertisers and investors, he has turned down millions of dollars. In the early days of the company, Newmark decided Craigslist's mission would be to serve the community, not to make profits. That purpose is reflected in the company's motto: "Give people a break."[3]

Likewise, Newmark has ignored suggestions for changing the site's appearance to make it more flashy and modern. Craigslist looks like it did in the early days, using plain type and few graphics. The changes that have been made have improved the site's usefulness, such as making it available in more places and in more languages. These updates were suggested by

"A break from how difficult our lives are. It's like, if you're walking out of your apartment building and somebody is coming the other way with an armful of groceries, you hold the door. It feels good—it's the neighborly thing to do. And our species survives by cooperating."[4]

—*Craig Newmark on the meaning of Craigslist's motto, "Give people a break."*

the site's users, not industry observers and critics. According to Newmark, "Basically our whole site is based on what people have asked for. We've had very few ideas of our own."[5]

Not even the size of Craigslist's staff has changed much over the years. This is unusual, considering the company's tremendous growth. When Newmark started Craigslist, it had eight employees. As of 2010, it had 30. The company's headquarters is a Victorian house in San Francisco—the same house where Newmark moved the business after it outgrew his living room. Newmark continues to work at home some of the time, particularly early mornings and late evenings. At the company's headquarters, he shares an office with Buckmaster. The two men's desks are set up so they work back to back, ensuring they will not distract one another.

In another early decision, Newmark allowed Craigslist users to post and view nearly all ads free of charge. In his opinion, everyone should have access to the Internet. "The Internet is about inclusion," he has said. "On the Net, no one should be left out."[6] To stop people from posting too many ads and otherwise misusing the site, Craigslist charges fees for certain kinds of ads in certain locations. For instance, in 17 US cities, a fee of $25 is charged to place a job ad; the fee is $75 in San Francisco. And in New York City, listing an apartment costs $10.

Allowing users to self-publish and self-police their postings reflects the culture of trust Newmark has created on his site. He believes people should treat others as they want to be treated, and he insists that much of his success has come from living according to basic human values. Newmark has said repeatedly that people are trustworthy and good.

THE DOT-COM BUST

Even more quickly than the dot-com bubble or boom developed, it went bust. Between 2000 and 2002, hundreds of dot-com companies went bankrupt, and many more lost large sums of money.

According to business analysts, the primary reason for the dot-com bust was that billions of dollars were invested in companies run by people with little or no business sense or experience. Investors, owners, and employees were all eager to make a lot of money from their companies, but they did not necessarily have a solid vision or plan for doing so.

A second reason for the dot-coms' failure was that they moved too quickly. Many tried to be first online with a service or product. This resulted in their spending a lot of money in a short amount of time and without much planning.

A third reason for the bust was that doing business online was completely new. Some investors were so excited about owning part of an online business that they put their money into any Internet company. Many online companies focused on attracting young customers by using flashy Web sites and clever offers. However, these companies often failed to follow through by delivering high-quality products and customer service.

COMPANY EARNINGS AND VALUE

Craigslist is a privately held company, which

means it does not have to publicize its earnings. Industry experts believe the company has been profitable since 1999—the year Newmark set it up as a corporation. In 2009, the estimated costs of running the company were $6 million, and the estimated earnings were $100 million. That left $94 million in profits. Earnings were up 23 percent from the year before, and 1,000 percent over the past five years. Most of the earnings are believed to come from the fees charged to place job ads.

Some experts have suggested that if Craigslist were to accept paid advertising and charge all users for posting ads, it could earn $550 million a year. And if the company were sold, some speculate the likely price tag would be $1 billion.

Newmark refuses to confirm estimates of the company's earnings and value. He responds to questions about these topics with wry answers such as:

CRAIGSLIST'S EMPLOYEES

The fact that Craigslist has only 30 employees is amazing, given the company's tremendous growth and worldwide presence. This fact is even more amazing, however, when considered in comparison to the number of employees at other popular Web sites. For instance, Google, the most popular site among Americans, has almost 20,000 employees. And eBay, which is similar in popularity to Craigslist, has just over 16,000. Craigslist has controlled the number of employees it has needed, largely by not having a marketing staff. Craigslist's employees are programmers, accountants, and customer service providers.

"Our philosophy is that we're basically making enough money to pay the bills, with a little left."[7] He also insists that Craigslist is not interested in making money; rather, the company's goal is to serve the community.

Many leaders of online companies shared this goal at the beginning of the dot-com boom, which lasted from approximately 1995 to 2000. During this short era, thousands of online companies were started, built up through huge investment, and then sold for incredible profit. Well-known examples of such companies are eBay and Google.

Newmark could have followed this course but resisted. As he told one interviewer,

> I admit that when I think of the money one could make from all this, I get a little twinge. But I'm pretty happy with nerd values: Get yourself a comfortable living, then do a little something to change the world.[8] +

Newmark has been honored by *Time* magazine as one of the world's
100 most influential people.

As the president and CEO, Buckmaster deals with different issues that arise on Craigslist.

PROVIDING CUSTOMER SERVICE

Newmark's belief in the importance of providing good customer service reflects, in part, his own experience working for big companies. In most big companies, according to Newmark, employees are not honest with their managers. Rather, they tell their managers what they think the managers want to hear. In Newmark's words, "A lot of chief executives . . . are surrounded by people who filter things so much that they have no idea of what is really happening."[1] Newmark prefers to be a hands-on executive—one who is directly involved in what is going on at his company.

Usually, half of Newmark's 14-hour day is spent providing customer service. He begins and ends every day at his home computer, responding to customers' e-mails. He also answers e-mails on and off throughout the day at Craigslist's headquarters, finding time between meetings, meals, and public appearances.

Many of the e-mails are customers' complaints about problems with posting and responding to ads on the Web site. Solving these problems is straightforward—even dull—in many situations, but in others, it

LOST WORKER PRODUCTIVITY FROM SPAMMING

A March 2009 report by McAfee Labs, which does research on computer security, estimated that the average worker gets 45 spam-type e-mails per day. On average, 43 of these e-mails are prevented from being delivered by spam-filtering software. Handling the two spam e-mails that do get through and then getting back to work takes the worker about 50 seconds. If the worker makes $30 per hour, the cost to the employer of the worker responding to spam is about 50 cents per day. Over a year, the cost of dealing with spam is $182.50 per employee. For a large company, this results in huge costs.

involves a fair amount of detective work. Newmark compares it to being a forensic crime solver, similar to the detectives on the *CSI* programs on television.

FIGHTING SPAMMERS

Craigslist and other advertising and sales Web sites are plagued by two general kinds of problems. The first is spamming, which involves the abuse of electronic messaging, such as e-mail. A spammer sends a huge number of messages to people at random, without their having requested them. In one common type of spamming, so-called e-mail harvesters gather the e-mail addresses of people who post ads on Craigslist. The harvesters then sell the e-mail addresses to businesses that send out their own messages to Craigslist users. Many of these businesses are illegitimate and try to involve users in activities such as pornography and fraud.

Spammers also post phony job applications on the site. After job hunters fill out and return the applications, they receive countless unwanted e-mails. Interestingly, some of the messages sent by spammers encourage Craigslist users to try other Web sites offering similar services. The messages say things such as "we're better than craigslist, why don't you use us instead."[2] Newmark makes a point of contacting these spammers himself. In many situations, being contacted directly by Craig Newmark, the founder of Craigslist, is enough to make the spammers stop.

On the Craigslist Online Community site, a page about the company's efforts to fight spam includes this statement: "We devote a LOT of time and energy to combating these evils, but it's a never-ending battle."[3] Newmark and his customer service team are always looking for new methods of controlling spamming. Some methods involve technological tools that prevent harvesting and refuse to accept

KINDS OF E-MAIL SCAMS

In years past, many online scams used viruses and spyware to get information from people's computers. Today, scams involving e-mail are more common, including the following:

• Phishing is a type of scam that asks people to provide personal information, such as the numbers and passwords to bank accounts or credit cards. The requests come from sources that seem legitimate but are phony, such as scammers pretending to be banks or credit card companies.

• Money-handling scams involve using an outside person to receive money obtained from a previous scam. For a small reward, that person puts the money in another account before the scammer transfers it elsewhere, usually overseas. Involving another person makes it hard for law enforcement officials to identify the original source of the money—the scammer.

• In a lottery scam, the victim is told he or she has won a large sum of money in a foreign lottery. To receive the money, the victim must pay a small fee or provide access to his or her bank account.

• An Internet auction scam asks someone bidding on an item on a legitimate Web site, such as eBay, to make a deal outside the site. For instance, the bidder may be promised a reduced price if he or she pays a fee, usually in cash, before closing the deal.

A HISTORIC SCAM

One common scam has a long history, originating in the 1500s, when it was called the Spanish Prisoner. A confidence man, or scammer, told the mark, or victim, he represented someone wealthy. That person was wrongly being held prisoner in Spain but could not reveal his true identity without being harmed. The confidence man asked the mark to pay a ransom to win the prisoner's release. After being released, the prisoner would pay the mark a generous reward and let the mark marry his beautiful daughter. The success of this scam depended on the mark's willingness to keep the plot a secret.

duplicate and multiple postings by one source. Other methods include requiring a valid telephone number and e-mail account with each posting and asking users to report cases of spamming.

FIGHTING SCAMMERS

The second kind of problem faced by Craigslist and similar Web sites is scamming. Scamming involves various types of fraud, in which people are tricked or cheated out of possessions or money. For example, some scammers pretend to offer college loans and get students to provide confidential information, such as their Social Security or bank account number.

Many of the cases of fraud seen by Newmark and Craigslist's customer service team have the same basic qualities. For example, the ad is posted by someone who says he or she lives far away—

Deven Trabosh offered the chance to marry her and buy her house in a posting on Craigslist.

often, out of the country. In addition, an exchange of money is involved before the item or service advertised is actually provided. Payments from the scammer are made with a fake check or other form of payment. Finally, delivery of the product or service is complicated. For instance, delivery might involve traveling to another country or having to use a shipping company that is unreliable or does not even exist.

On the Craigslist site, a page about scams warns users against responding to ads with these qualities. Users are advised to deal with people in their local area, whom they can meet in person. Users are also warned against taking or paying money in advance of a transaction. Deals that sound too good to be true usually involve fraud, according to the Web page.

REAL ESTATE ADS: SCAMS AND CLUTTERING

Craigslist's customer service team deals with many real estate scams, too. Particularly common are so-called bait-and-switch scams, in which the seller advertises one thing but delivers another. In one such scam, a scammer posted an ad offering to rent out a house he did not even own. The house was for sale, and the scammer had obtained information about it from a real estate ad. In the Craigslist ad, he offered to rent out the house for a ridiculously low monthly fee. When would-be renters responded, the scammer asked them for a security deposit, a significant sum of money paid to secure the rental. The scam went undetected until the real estate agent listing the house got calls from the scammed renters. This scam has been discovered in Kentucky, Florida, and New York.

A lot of the real estate scams linked to Craigslist involve apartment listings in New York City, where apartments are in high demand. To discourage scammers, in 2006, Craigslist started charging a fee of ten dollars for each ad for a brokered apartment posted on the New York site.

Charging a fee for apartment rental ads was also intended to stop people from posting too many of these kinds of ads on Craigslist. These ads clutter the site, in Newmark's opinion, making it hard for users to find what they are looking for.

"On our site, the number of bad guys is very tiny. Nevertheless, the bad guys are persistent."[5]

—*Craig Newmark*

Newmark gets impatient with people who post a lot of new ads but do not remove the old ones. In one case, someone in New York City e-mailed Newmark about a woman there who was posting more than 25 new real estate ads per day. Despite being annoyed, Newmark decided not to be too hard on her; he removed 100 of her ads but left others.

Newmark has also made personal visits to some realtors' offices, speaking to them face to face about their Craigslist violations. When people realize who he is, they tend to respond in much the same way. "The usual response is panic," says Newmark, "followed by photography. Somebody whips out a camera. Often several cameras."[4]

FLAGGING SUSPICIOUS ADS

Newmark and his customer service team do not actually screen or review the postings on Craigslist. Rather, they rely on self-policing among users. Users are asked to flag suspicious ads and to report them to customer service. When an ad has been flagged several times, Newmark and his team review it and often delete it. For example, one Craigslist ad offered a very nice car for sale at a price well below its actual value. Users flagged the ad, sensing that it involved some kind of scam. The customer service team removed the ad within ten hours of its posting. Similar ads placed over the next few days were deleted within two hours.

"People can see that when they report a problem to us, we take it seriously," says Newmark. "We want life to be fair, even though it's not."[6] +

A scammer used Craigslist to try to collect deposits for an apartment in this building in New York City.

A rental home was stripped after a fake ad posted on Craigslist invited people to take whatever they wanted.

DEALING WITH CRIME

Working in customer service has led Newmark to conclude, "Our experience every day is that people are overwhelmingly trustworthy and good. There are bad guys out there. There are not many of them, although they make a lot of noise, so people think there are more bad guys than there are. . . . My team and I, we go after them every day."[1]

More and more bad guys have been using Craigslist, it seems, and the media has focused closely on reporting their crimes. Law enforcement agencies have asked for Craigslist's help in solving many crimes, but they also have been critical of some of the company's efforts at prevention.

ROBBERIES AND BURGLARIES

Police in Brooklyn, New York, arrested four men who used Craigslist to arrange meetings with people and then rob them. The men posted an ad offering sales of iPhones in large quantities at a good price. Interested buyers were told when and where to meet. When they arrived, they were robbed of their cash and possessions. The police set up

STING OPERATIONS

In law enforcement, a sting operation is a plan that uses deception to catch someone committing a crime. In a typical sting, a police officer plays the role of a potential victim. The officer sets up a situation to become involved with a criminal and then goes along with the illegal activity—all the while gathering evidence of the crime. Some police officers pose as criminals in sting operations, pretending to participate in crimes. Police must be careful, however, to avoid entrapment, which is luring or tricking someone into committing a crime. Entrapment is illegal in the United States.

a sting operation: they posed as buyers and then caught the robbers in the middle of their crime.

Police in Chicago, Illinois, used a similar sting operation to solve a string of robberies tied to Craigslist ads. One of the officers on the case called this type of crime "robbery by appointment."[2]

In Seattle, Washington, an unusual home burglary was tied to a Craigslist ad that read, "Home being demolished. Come and take whatever you want, nothing is off limits."[3] The ad also provided the address of the home—a rental property that was unoccupied at the time. Within a week,

COMPUTER FORENSICS

The word *forensics* refers to the science or technology used to establish evidence in a court of law. Many people have become familiar with forensics from watching the *CSI* programs on television. The abbreviation *CSI* means crime scene investigation. At a crime scene, common types of forensic evidence are fingerprints and samples of fibers, blood, and hair.

Computer forensics involves looking for evidence on a computer. Much of this evidence includes materials created or saved on the computer, such as financial records, photographs, and e-mails. These can usually be located even if they have been hidden on or deleted from the computer. Locating other kinds of evidence involves tracking the computer user's activities, such as browsing the Internet and sending and receiving e-mails. Specialized software and training are needed to find much of this evidence.

Computer forensics can provide evidence in many kinds of legal cases. For example, financial records might be used as evidence of embezzlement, in which an employee steals money from an employer. Copying or deleting computer files might be used as evidence of industrial espionage, in which someone steals or destroys confidential information about a company's products or operations.

everything in the home had been taken—including the kitchen sink. The owner was stunned. She had not posted the ad. The police, working with Craigslist, traced the ad to a woman whose mother had been evicted from the rental. In fact, Craigslist users had flagged the ad as suspicious within hours of its posting.

Newmark is eager to help law enforcement officials solve crimes. On average, he is asked for help once a week by local police officers or FBI agents. In his words,

> We actively go after crooks by working with the police. Anything that is criminal is just not okay on our site. . . . We know how to help the cops with the simple forensics they need on our site.[4]

Doing so means providing the police with information about users' e-mail addresses.

OTHER CRIMES

Many of the crimes connected to Craigslist have involved ads placed in the category Erotic Services. Although the category is intended for adults looking for consensual sexual activity, it frequently contains ads for prostitution. Because prostitution is illegal in every state except Nevada, the ads cannot specifically offer sexual services for money. Instead, they offer services such as massages and paid escorts, or dates, assuming that people who use the category know what is actually intended.

By concentrating on these kinds of Craigslist ads, police in New York City, San Francisco, Seattle, and Chicago have increased their arrests of prostitutes, along with the men who contact them. Crimes involving children, such as kidnapping and sexual abuse, have received special attention. More arrests have been made for related crimes, such as selling drugs and carrying guns.

Several murders have also been linked to ads placed in the Erotic Services category. In the most well-publicized case, a 25-year-old woman was shot and killed in a Boston hotel in April 2009. When police examined her home computer, they discovered she had posted an ad for massage services on Craigslist. She also had exchanged e-mails with the man who killed her, which allowed police to identify him. One detective said the killer's use of his e-mail address to contact the victim "was like leaving the gun at the scene with your fingerprints on the gun."[5]

Within days, police were able to tie the killer to two more attacks of young women in area hotels. Like the murder victim, these women had posted ads in the Erotic Services category on Craigslist. Both had been robbed at gunpoint but not killed. Nevertheless, when the media realized the connection among the crimes, they started calling the murderer the "Craigslist killer."

These crimes occurred just weeks before a memorial service for an earlier murder victim. A 24-year-old Minneapolis woman had been killed in October 2007 after responding to a Craigslist ad for a job as a nanny. Newmark had responded personally to this tragedy, contacting the young woman's family and working with them for over a year to sponsor a memorial concert for her. Newmark attended the memorial in May 2009. While there, he made this statement:

Despite the billions of times that well-meaning people have helped each other through Craigslist, it's been devastating to see that it can also be used

THE CRAIGSLIST KILLER

Police were shocked when they learned the Craigslist killer, Philip Markoff, was a 23-year-old medical school student at Boston University. They learned his name by tracing the e-mails he had exchanged with the murder victim. Next, they determined his home address. But police were not sure what Markoff looked like. They identified a suspect by reviewing security videos from the hotels at which the three women were attacked. Police officers waited outside Markoff's apartment building. Within a day, they knew they had found the killer. Markoff committed suicide in jail in August 2010 while awaiting his trial, which was scheduled to begin in March 2011.

Philip Markoff used Craigslist to lure his murder victim to his hotel room.

by bad people to take cruel advantage of others and bring a senseless end to a beautiful young life.[6]

PREVENTING CRIMES

To try to prevent crimes such as these, Newmark and others at Craigslist have worked with law enforcement agencies across the United States. The company has placed restrictions on ads that might draw people into dangerous or illegal situations.

Ads posted in Erotic Services have received particular attention. In 2008, after the first murder related to the site, Craigslist took several steps intended to discourage people from posting problem ads. First, the company required each person who posted an Erotic Services ad to provide a phone number. Next, the company required use of a credit card for payment. Having this information allowed Craigslist staff to confirm the identity of each person who posted such an ad. According to Newmark, adding these requirements was effective. Within the first year, the number of ads placed in the category dropped by 90 to 95 percent.

In May 2009, after the Craigslist killer's crime spree in Boston, Craigslist started charging

HELPING CHILDREN

One of the organizations Craigslist has worked with to prevent criminal activity on the Web site is the National Center for Missing and Exploited Children (NCMEC). This organization has three goals: (1) to help prevent children from being kidnapped and sexually abused; (2) to help find children who are missing; and (3) to provide assistance to these children, as well as their families and the professionals who work with them. Although the NCMEC is a private organization, its mission is mandated, or empowered, by the US Congress, and it works with federal law enforcement agencies such as the FBI.

a fee of ten dollars to place an ad in the Erotic Services category. All the money would be donated to charity. Under pressure to do more, the company shut down this category and replaced it with one called Adult Services. Hoping to prevent the same problems from occurring, Craigslist established strict review policies for ads. It also promised to add enough employees to review the ads posted in this new category and to enforce the new policies.

Still, criticism of Craigslist has continued. Many people have argued that renaming the category did not solve the problems associated with it. Others suggested that Craigslist acted too much on its own, rather than working directly with law enforcement. Some critics claimed that Craigslist was promoting prostitution and profiting from the sales of Adult Services ads. Some even accused Newmark and the company of being partly responsible for the crimes that had occurred.

Criticism of Craigslist peaked in late August 2010, when attorneys general in 17 states demanded that the Web site shut down the Adult Services category. They claimed the site was still not doing enough to review postings and block potentially illegal or dangerous ads. Human rights groups that focus on protecting women and children from abuse agreed with this claim and demanded that Craigslist take action. Additional pressure came from the US House of Representatives, which scheduled a September 15 hearing to look into how criminal activity is conducted using Web sites such as Craigslist.

On September 3, Craigslist bowed to the pressure: It blocked users' access to the Adult Services category on all of its US Web sites. And on September 15, at the US House of Representatives hearing, Craigslist's director of customer service and law enforcement relations, William "Clint" Powell, stated that the company had no plans to reinstate the category. This decision to censor content left people in law enforcement, the media, and the Internet industry wondering how Craigslist and other Web sites would be affected—now and in the future.

"We aren't comfortable with any crime happening on Craigslist. . . . We are going to keep working and adopting new measures until we get that off the site."[7]

—*Jim Buckmaster*

Newmark has stated repeatedly that Craigslist cannot control how people use the Web site. "People might use our site, much like they might use the phone, or a car, or the roads," he has said, "and I can't find a reason for any of us to feel guilty about it."[8] He has also pointed out that, considering the millions of people who use the site every month, the level of crime is really quite low. Through all the criticism and controversy, Newmark has remained committed to preventing people from using Craigslist for illegal purposes. +

Connecticut Attorney General Richard Blumenthal demanded the Adult
Services section of Craigslist be shut down.

Newspapers have continued to face financial troubles as classified ad sales have declined.

FACING THE COMPETITION

Not everyone is pleased with the tremendous success of Craigslist. Competing businesses, in particular, are trying to determine how Craigslist has done so well in such a short amount of time. Some are unhappy about the earnings they have lost to Craigslist, while others are eager to capture some of the business the Web site has attracted. More and more, Newmark finds himself in the position of defending the company he founded and built.

STRUGGLING NEWSPAPERS

Many people in the newspaper industry are frustrated, even angry, with Craigslist, because it has taken away much of their business selling classified advertisements. Industry analysts report that in the past, many large, big-city newspapers brought in up to half their earnings by selling classified ads.

Many of these newspapers now offer online listings of classified ads. In fact, sales of online ads have increased greatly in recent years. Unfortunately for newspapers, most of that increase has gone to Craigslist. Some in the newspaper industry have called Craigslist the "newspaper killer"[1] and the "destroyer of journalism."[2]

NETWORK EFFECTS

Craigslist benefits from what economists and technology researchers call network effects. People are drawn to Craigslist because it is bigger, and therefore buyers are more likely to find what they are seeking and sellers are more likely to find a buyer for their goods and services. Network effects are common on the Internet: being bigger draws more users, which then makes a popular site such as Craigslist more attractive to newcomers. Network effects make it difficult for other companies to displace market leaders.

In defense of Craigslist, Newmark points to Web sites that specialize in certain kinds of classified ads. For instance, Monster.com, the largest employment Web site in the world, has approximately 1 million job ads posted at any time. Compared to Craigslist, Newmark argues, specialty sites take away significantly more business from newspapers than Craigslist does.

Newmark recognizes newspapers are losing money. But he feels putting all or most of the blame on Craigslist is scapegoating. In his opinion, "The newspapers have a lot of problems these days."[3]

DECLINING NEWSPAPER CIRCULATION

A 2009 study of newspaper sales, or circulation, gathered information from 1,400 daily newspapers in the United States. It found that today, only one in eight Americans buys the newspaper every day, compared to one in three Americans in 1940. Sales have been declining since 1987, as newspapers have faced greater competition for readership and advertising.

Between April and September 2009, most of the nation's largest newspapers reported large drops in circulation. The nation's largest newspaper, *USA Today*, lost 17 percent. This loss dropped the paper into second place in terms of circulation. The *Wall Street Journal* took over first place and actually showed a 1 percent increase in circulation.

Especially hard hit was the *San Francisco Chronicle*, which lost nearly 26 percent of its daily readers. This was the biggest loss reported by a major US newspaper. Compared to newspapers in other parts of the country, those in the San Francisco area have shown greater declines in circulation.

When asked how Craigslist's success has damaged the newspaper industry, Newmark said, "Somebody invented recently a myth that we're hurting newspapers. I've done a lot of research. That appears to be an invention. . . . We're a minor factor."[4]

One of those problems is the current state of the newspaper industry. Today, few newspapers are independently and locally owned, as they were in the past. Rather, most are owned by one of several large national companies. In contrast to past owners, these companies expect their newspapers to make big profits.

Another major problem facing newspapers is the decline in readership. Research has shown that newspaper sales are at their lowest level in 70 years. Some readers have gone online to read the daily newspaper, but in most cases, the effect is the same: they are not paying to read the newspaper.

Young people, especially, are no longer reading newspaper ads. Instead, they are going online, preferring to use a Web site such as Craigslist to buy and sell things. Newmark suggests that many, if not most, of the people who post ads on Craigslist would never consider placing an ad in a newspaper.

Newmark also suggests that people like these represent the future of journalism. He supports what he calls citizen journalism, in which everyday people write and publish materials online. This form of journalism is clearly quite different from the traditional form, in which professionals write and edit articles and then have them published in newspapers. Newmark envisions a blending of the two forms. He believes that combination would make news reporting more serious and trustworthy.

COMPETING WEB SITES

Many companies would like to capture some of the business of online classified advertising. In 2010, that business was estimated to be worth $22 billion. Microsoft, America Online, Yahoo! Google, eBay, Facebook, MySpace, and Twitter have all created new Web sites of classified ads or have placed ads on their existing sites.

So far, none of these sites has succeeded in taking away business from Craigslist. On the contrary, Craigslist has continued to grow. Not only has the Web site attracted new users, but its existing users have grown even more loyal in response to the increase in competition.

Even so, two sites have drawn attention. Oodle was launched in 2004 with an estimated $20 million in investors' money. Users can post ads on the Web site for free, or they can pay to have extra features that will bring more attention to their ads. Oodle is called an aggregator, which means it collects and combines classified ads from other sites. It has partnered with more than 200 businesses and organizations, ranging from Walmart to Facebook to the US armed services. Using this partnering approach, Oodle has established itself in the business of online classifieds and continues to grow. Still, Craigslist draws more individual users.

The second Web site, Kijiji, was launched internationally in 2005 and in the United States in 2007. It is highly similar to Craigslist in terms of being organized by country and city and having many categories of classified ads. Kijiji does not allow any sexual content on the site, however, and it has pledged to strictly control spamming and scamming on the site. The major difference between Craigslist and Kijiji is that Kijiji intends to earn profits. Although the site allows users to post ads for free, it

KIJIJI POPULAR IN CANADA

Kijiji is the most popular free classified ads Web site in Canada and the nation's twelfth most popular site overall. Each month, almost 9 million Canadians visit Kijiji to look for apartments, cars, boats, and other items, as well as to exchange opinions. To date, Kijiji Web sites are available in 99 Canadian cities, coast to coast, and each site uses the city's local language. For this reason, Kijiji is especially popular in the French-speaking regions of Canada, such as Quebec.

eBay launched the Web site Kijiji to offer free classified ads.

accepts paid advertising from outside companies—
something Craigslist has always refused to do.

Kijiji is owned by eBay, a well-known auction
Web site. Soon after it launched Kijiji, eBay boasted
it would become the number-one classified ads site
in the United States. But after approximately
18 months, this had not happened. In fact, the

new site had attracted only 10 percent of the number of people using Craigslist. Hoping to increase business by drawing on the eBay name, the company changed the name of the US site to eBay Classifieds in March 2010.

Craigslist remains the leader in the fast-growing business of online classified ads. Newmark has identified several key factors for the Web site's success:

> We're a very simple, effective site. It doesn't hurt to be free. And, we have a pretty good culture of trust going. That means that I am committed to customer service.[5]

GOING TO COURT

Interestingly, eBay also owns part of Craigslist. The purchase occurred in 2004, when a former Craigslist employee sold his shares of the company's stock to eBay. When Newmark was asked about the sale, he said,

> We tried to channel it toward a partner we could live with, with a similar moral compass. It was not my intention to have any of this happen, but we're happy with the results.[6]

BUCKMASTER'S VIEW OF THE COMPETITION

When asked about Craigslist's competition, Buckmaster said the company is less concerned with attracting new users and more concerned with serving current users. In his words, "Craigslist as you see it today is the result of millions of suggestions received from tens of millions of users, and the features you see are those which Craigslist's users have asked for. We're simply trying to follow through on feedback received from our users."[7]

According to Newmark, Craigslist hoped to use eBay's resources to help fight spamming and scamming on the site and to expand it to even more countries. eBay executives had assured him the company was happy to be a minority owner, and they had not mentioned plans to buy or create similar Web sites.

Within a year, the two companies were at odds. eBay was reportedly impatient with how long it was taking Craigslist to approve a plan for international expansion. And Craigslist had become suspicious of eBay after learning it had bought several international classified ad sites and launched Kijiji. Two years later, Craigslist became concerned about protecting its interests when eBay launched Kijiji in the United States, becoming a direct competitor.

In April 2008, eBay filed a lawsuit against Craigslist. It accused the company of issuing Newmark and Buckmaster additional shares of stock in Craigslist, thus increasing their level of ownership while reducing that of eBay. Doing so prevented eBay from having one of its executives sit on Craigslist's board of directors and participate in decision making.

One month later, Craigslist filed a countersuit against eBay. It accused eBay of using confidential information about Craigslist to develop a competing Web site. Craigslist also claimed that eBay had not been honest about its plans to start its own site. A statement released by Craigslist said, "Sadly, we have an uncomfortably conflicted shareholder in our midst, one that is obsessed with dominating online classifieds for the purpose of maximizing its own profits."[8]

The two companies went to court in December 2009. In September 2010, a judge ruled on the case. Judge William B. Chandler III's ruling did not seem

ANOTHER SIGN OF SUCCESS

During the week of March 13, 2009, Craigslist replaced MySpace as the most searched-for term on the Internet. MySpace had been the most searched-for term for the previous three years. Some of the increased popularity of Craigslist was linked to the economic downturn in the United States. More and more people became interested in making money by selling their belongings and in saving money by buying used items, and more people used the Web site's job postings to look for employment after they were laid off.

to create a decisive winner in the case. On one hand, the court invalidated the reorganizing of shares Newmark and Buckmaster had made. This decision prompted eBay to claim victory. However, Chandler ruled in favor of Craigslist in terms of staggering board elections. This will make it difficult for eBay to appoint someone to the board of directors. This will also limit eBay's access to confidential information about Craigslist and its influence in major company decisions.

But this decision did not end the legal battles between the two Internet companies. The ruling was made on the case filed in April 2008. In November of 2010, the two companies remained in conflict as they awaited a decision on the case Craigslist filed against eBay in May 2008. +

Newmark testified at the trial between Craigslist and eBay on December 9, 2009.

Debbie Diamond found nine possible kidney donors for her husband, Neil, through a posting on Craigslist.

SERVING THE COMMUNITY

Most media reports about Craigslist have covered negative topics. These topics have included the Web site's harmful effect on the newspaper industry, its legal battle with eBay over ownership, and the crimes linked to ads posted on the site. Far less attention has been paid to the many positive ways people have used Craigslist and to Newmark's personal commitment to serving the community.

HELPING PEOPLE CONNECT

In addition to buying and selling on Craigslist, people turn to the Web site to give and receive help. Newmark has said, "People are smart, good and surprise me with the way they use our site."[1]

People's use of the Free category on Craigslist has changed, reflecting the tough economic times in the United States. In the past, this category usually contained postings about items people want to give away. But in recent years, it has included increasingly more ads from people asking for financial support.

Other people have asked Craigslist users for help by posting ads in the Lost+Found category. For instance, one woman left her iPod on a train. When she realized what she had done, she immediately posted an ad on Craigslist. The man who found the iPod was a regular Craigslist user. So, when he arrived home from the train, he immediately checked the Web site. He found the woman's ad, contacted her, and returned the lost item.

HURRICANE KATRINA

Hurricane Katrina hit the southeastern coast of Louisiana on August 29, 2005. Katrina was the costliest hurricane in US history, causing $81 billion in damage from central Florida across the Gulf Coast to Texas. In New Orleans, an estimated 80 percent of the city was flooded because of the almost total failure of the city's levees, which had been built to contain two major bodies of water: the Mississippi River and Lake Pontchartrain. Katrina was also one of the deadliest hurricanes in US history, killing approximately 1,800 people. Most of the deaths occurred in New Orleans, where people drowned.

People have also turned to Craigslist in times of disaster. Just days after Hurricane Katrina pounded New Orleans, Louisiana, the city's Craigslist site filled with ads. Survivors used the site to let family and friends know where they were going, and family and friends used it to find missing loved ones. During the weeks and months after the hurricane, people continued to post ads offering housing, food, and jobs to survivors. Craigslist staff also worked with volunteers to make the best use of the 40 computers set up at the Superdome, the stadium where an estimated 30,000 people gathered during and after the hurricane.

Newmark was impressed with how the people of New Orleans found new and creative ways to use Craigslist. He remarked, "Sometimes you have to know when to get out of the way and let your community take control as much as possible."[2]

ORGANIZING THE COMMUNITY

Although providing customer service is his primary job, Newmark has also become increasingly involved in serving the community. He feels doing so is one of his responsibilities as the founder and chairperson of Craigslist. Having the time and money to serve is the greatest benefit of the company's success, in Newmark's opinion. Craigslist reportedly gives 1 percent of its profits to charity.

Because Craigslist has never focused on earning big profits, many people assume it is a nonprofit organization. Newmark considered making Craigslist a nonprofit in its early days, when he ran it with a group of volunteers. He eventually decided against this because of the kinds of laws involved in operating a nonprofit group. In Newmark's mind, Craigslist is neither a for-profit nor a nonprofit but rather something in between. He has said, "There is no term to describe what we do. On paper, we're a for-profit. But we just don't run like that."[3]

Newmark believes strongly in the idea of a culture of participation, in which everyone does his or her part to support and improve the community. In his opinion, Americans have always been eager to serve. He also believes using the Internet is the ideal way to make people aware of what needs to be done and to encourage them to get involved.

His experience with Craigslist has demonstrated the effectiveness of working within the Internet community.

As the founder and chairperson of Craigslist, Newmark has a lot of power and influence. Many people would like him to become involved in their causes. He is modest about that, however, and prefers to think of himself as something of a community organizer— making charitable opportunities available to others. In his words,

CRAIGSLIST.ORG

The final part of a Web address is called an extension. Different extensions are used to indicate different kinds of sites. The extension .com is most common; it means commercial. Other commonly used extensions are .gov for government, .edu for education, and .mil for military.

Craigslist's Web address ends with .org, the extension used almost exclusively by nonprofit organizations. A nonprofit works to benefit a certain group or to support a certain issue. Its primary mission is to provide service, not to make profits. Nonprofit organizations do raise money through donations and fund-raising. Most of that money goes toward fulfilling the group's mission, but some of it is used to run the organization. A nonprofit must be registered in the state in which it is based and must operate according to that state's laws.

Craigslist has always used the .org extension to emphasize its purpose of providing service, not making profits. But doing so has sometimes led people to assume the company is a nonprofit. Newmark thought about making Craigslist a nonprofit in its early days. He decided against it, though, because of the legal requirements of running a nonprofit organization.

Like most humans, I'd like to save the world, but I figure I need a nap. So, I figured it'd be much easier to talk you into doing it by talking up the efforts of people who are really effective at helping others.[4]

THE CRAIGSLIST FOUNDATION

In 2000, a year after Newmark formed Craigslist as a corporation, he established the Craigslist Foundation, a nonprofit organization. Its purpose is "to connect people and organizations to the resources they need to strengthen communities and neighborhoods."[5] To achieve this purpose, the Craigslist Foundation offers training in areas such as marketing, technology, and fund-raising. Each year, for example, the foundation holds events called boot camps to bring people together and help them discover ways to build strong neighborhoods and communities. The foundation also holds discussion groups in cities across the United States. In these groups, people share their experiences with neighborhood and community projects and identify areas that still need attention.

Many people view the purpose of the Craigslist Foundation as providing help to other nonprofit organizations. For instance, within days of the earthquake in Haiti in January 2010, the foundation listed on its Web site six charitable organizations to which individuals could donate money. The site explained that each organization already had people and resources set up in Haiti. In addition, Craigslist provided a link to Google's Missing People Finder site to help individuals locate victims displaced by the disaster.

PUBLIC-PRIVATE PARTNERSHIPS

The best way to bring about change, Newmark believes, is to create public-private partnerships. A good example of such a partnership was formed in 2001 between Craigslist and schools in San Francisco. In the Wishlist Program for Schools and Non-Profits, teachers were asked to post on Craigslist lists of materials they needed for their students. People who wanted to help ordered these materials from local businesses and paid for them. The businesses then delivered the items to the schools. In all, the schools received approximately $30,000 worth of materials.

ALL FOR GOOD

In June 2009, inspired by President Obama's call for Americans to do volunteer work, Newmark started the Web site All For Good. This "Craigslist for service," as some have called it, was designed to connect people with projects and activities.[6] It is a database of volunteer opportunities all over the United States. Users can search the database by location, type of work, and other details to find people and organizations that need help.

The idea underlying All For Good is to make volunteer work easy and convenient for people. Newmark has said,

> Lots of people want to help out, but it has to be something doable, which means it might have to be nearby, and it has to be something you believe in.[7]

SUPPORTING VETERANS

Supporting US veterans is especially important to Newmark because of the sacrifices these individuals have made for their fellow Americans. Newmark has become involved in veterans' needs by serving on the board of directors of Iraq and Afghanistan Veterans of America. This organization helped pass a new GI Bill, which is legislation that provides medical and educational benefits to veterans. The group also helped veterans of the current military conflicts collect back pay for their service, which had been long delayed.

In February 2010, Newmark served on a panel looking for ways to improve the system for processing veterans' disability claims. He was asked to serve by the Department of Veterans Affairs (VA), the federal organization that supports US veterans and their families. As a member of the

"What I'm really trying to do is find really good efforts, get out the word on them, and get people to talk to each other."[9]

—*Craig Newmark*

panel, Newmark helped select ten improvements to be made from the more than 3,000 suggestions offered by VA employees nationwide. For Newmark, listening to the people actually doing the work seemed the best way to identify needed changes. Newmark later said, "In any large organization, the rank and file knows what's really going on and can do things a lot better. However, that doesn't get to top management normally."[8] +

Volunteers organized through Craigslist to bring holiday cards and gifts to patients in a VA hospital.

Newmark visits his favorite coffee shop in San Francisco daily.

LIFE TODAY

Newmark, now in his late fifties, says this is the best time of his life. He is successful and famous. He has built one of the most unique, influential, and valuable companies on the Internet. And he has done so mostly on his own terms, turning down countless people's suggestions and investments.

Because of the success of Craigslist, Newmark has received several significant awards and honors. In 2005, *Time* included him on its list of 100 people shaping the modern world, and in 2008, *Business Week* magazine named him one of the 25 most influential people on the Web. In 2010, the US government honored him with a Federal 100 award for his service to the VA. He has even had a day, October 10, dedicated to him in San Francisco.

Yet, what Newmark enjoys about being successful and famous is not the attention. Rather, he enjoys the influence he now has over issues that are important to him. Today, he is especially committed to making government more responsive and accountable to the people it serves. His efforts at promoting citizen journalism and supporting US veterans are part of this larger goal.

THE FEDERAL 100 AWARD

The Federal 100 award is given annually to people in business, education, and government who make important contributions to ways in which the US government buys, uses, and manages information technology (IT). Each year, the 100 winners are honored "for their risk-taking, vision and pioneering spirit in the federal IT community."[1] The award winners are nominated by readers of *Federal Computer Week* magazine and selected by a panel of IT leaders in the United States. In 2010, the 100 winners included 75 men and 25 women from across a wide range of professions, ethnicities, and ages.

Newmark likes the fact he is mostly unrecognized. Few people would be able to identify this short, slightly overweight, balding man as the founder and chairperson of Craigslist. He has said, "A lot of people think there is no Craig, . . . and I kind of like that."[2] Being unrecognized allows Newmark to go about his daily life much as he has since he moved to San Francisco in 1993.

DAILY LIFE

Newmark begins and ends most days working in his office at home, answering customers' e-mails. That home is in Cole Valley, a neighborhood in San Francisco next to Golden Gate Park. The Craigslist headquarters is in a nearby neighborhood called Inner Sunset.

After living in an apartment for many years, Newmark bought a small house in Cole Valley. His plan for remodeling the house revealed his priorities, according to one interviewer: two widescreen televisions had been installed before the wall separating the bedroom and bathroom had been finished.

A deck off Newmark's house overlooks a wooded area that is home to many kinds of birds.

Newmark has installed a number of bird feeders on the deck, as well as several just outside the window of his home office. He jokes about being able to be a bird-watcher without ever leaving the house. He has said, "I prefer nature come to me, rather than going to nature."[3] On his blog, he often provides photographs and live video of the birds. One spring, he used photos to keep readers informed about a nest of eggs hatching and baby birds learning to fly.

Newmark drives a Toyota Prius, which is a gas-electric hybrid. And because he is concerned about the environment, he does not like the idea of

NEWMARK'S NEIGHBORHOODS

Newmark spends much of his time in two San Francisco neighborhoods: Cole Valley and Inner Sunset. Cole Valley, where Newmark has lived for more than 15 years, is located in north central San Francisco, next to Golden Gate Park. Most of the area's residents are families and young professionals. The businesses within Cole Valley are mostly independently owned, not chain stores and franchises. Restaurants and coffee shops are especially common. Visitors to Cole Valley can take in a scenic view of San Francisco by climbing Tank Hill.

Inner Sunset is the location of the Craigslist headquarters. This neighborhood lies just west of Cole Valley. Inner Sunset is known for the ethnic mix of its residents. This mix reflects the history of the neighborhood, which became home to many immigrants in the late 1800s and early 1900s. Many graduate students live in the area today, because it is the location of the medical school of the University of California, San Francisco. The businesses in Inner Sunset are a mixture of independently owned and franchise restaurants and shops. Because Inner Sunset is just three miles (5 km) from the Pacific Ocean, it is often fogged in.

individuals owning and driving their own cars for every little errand. Newmark prefers to take public transportation around San Francisco. He buys a monthly pass that allows him to ride the buses, trains, and cable cars that are part of the city's public transportation system.

Newmark frequently walks around his Cole Valley neighborhood—mostly on the advice of his nutritionist. He has lost 15 pounds (7 kg) by walking and using a pedometer to record the number of steps he takes every day. To treat the dogs he meets along the way, he often carries a bag of beef jerky in his pocket.

For many years, Newmark has made a daily visit to his favorite coffee shop, the Reverie Café. While there, he has coffee, looks over several newspapers and magazines, and chats with the other regular customers. Meeting friends at the café is one of his favorite leisure activities. He also met the architect who remodeled his house there.

Newmark's other favorite activities are reading, listening to music, and watching TV. He reads one or two books a week, many of which are mystery novels. He believes this type of book "offers insight into the way people work. That doesn't come naturally to me, as a nerd."[4] His favorite author is Lindsey

Davis, whose main character is a detective in ancient Rome. Newmark also reads books about trends, such as blogging and the media. His favorite musicians include Leonard Cohen, Tori Amos, and Sarah McLachlan. His favorite television shows are detective series: *Law and Order* and *CSI*.

In recent years, Newmark's routine life in Cole Valley has been disrupted more and more by traveling. With his status and influence have come requests to participate in meetings, speak at college graduations, and give advice to government agencies. Newmark often leaves home for a week at a time, attending several events per trip. Doing so has forced him to divide his time between providing customer service at Craigslist and serving in these other roles.

KEEPING A LOW PROFILE

As one of the owners of Craigslist, Newmark certainly has a lot of money. He does not live like a wealthy man, however. Before he

NEWMARK'S BLOG

Below the title of Newmark's blog, *cnewmark*, is the following line: "craig from craigslist indulges himself."[5] Newmark indulges himself by blogging about many different topics, ranging from social and political issues to personal interests. One time, he used his blog to involve readers in selecting his new eyeglasses. He had taken photographs of himself in several different styles of glasses and put them on his blog. Then, he asked readers to view the photos and vote on the best style. He also e-mailed the photos to friends, asking for their advice.

bought his Toyota Prius, Newmark drove a Saturn for ten years. When he bought a house, he selected one that was comfortable but small. And when he shopped for an MP3 player for a friend, he compared prices at several stores before he made a purchase.

When asked about how much money he has, Newmark avoids giving a specific answer. Instead, he gives clever responses such as "I am very comfortable. I can now afford a parking place, which is not often easy to get in San Francisco."[6]

Another reason for Newmark's unwillingness to discuss financial details seems to be his concern about personal security. Wealthy people are often the targets of kidnappers and terrorists. Newmark has given examples of people in positions similar to his, such as the owners of Google and eBay, who have surrounded themselves with security guards. He has said that wealth is burdensome.

Newmark will not likely ever live the life of the rich and famous. Instead, he has said, "My instincts tell me I could do more good following the path I have chosen."[7] Considering the success of Craigslist, as well as his own personal achievements, most people would agree. By remaining true to his basic values and vision, Craig Newmark has built both Craigslist and a community of Internet users. +

While Newmark is a successful business owner,
he still lives a relatively humble life.

TIMELINE

1952	1975	1976
On December 5, Craig Newmark is born in Morristown, New Jersey.	Newmark earns a bachelor's degree in computer science from Case Western Reserve University.	Newmark begins his 17-year career with IBM.

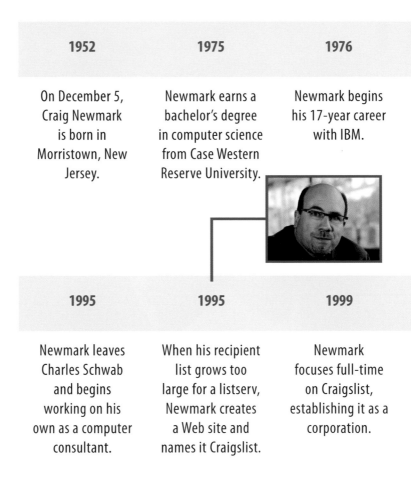

1995	1995	1999
Newmark leaves Charles Schwab and begins working on his own as a computer consultant.	When his recipient list grows too large for a listserv, Newmark creates a Web site and names it Craigslist.	Newmark focuses full-time on Craigslist, establishing it as a corporation.

1977	**1993**	**1995**
Newmark earns a master's degree in computer science from Case Western Reserve University.	After quitting his job at IBM, Newmark goes to work for Charles Schwab in San Francisco, California.	Newmark starts e-mailing friends and coworkers about events in San Francisco, then creates the listserv Craigslist.

1999	**2000**	**2000**
Newmark hires Jim Buckmaster to expand Craigslist and handle its technical operations.	Newmark makes Buckmaster the president and CEO of Craigslist; Newmark remains the chairperson and a customer service worker.	Newmark establishes the Craigslist Foundation, a nonprofit organization that helps strengthen neighborhoods and communities.

TIMELINE

2004	2004	2007
Craigslist is available in more than 30 cities.	In August, eBay buys part of Craigslist from a former Craigslist employee.	In June, eBay launches Kijiji in the United States, in direct competition with Craigslist.

2009	2009	2009
Craigslist is available in 700 cities in 70 countries and earns an estimated $100 million.	In mid-April, the Craigslist killer murders one woman and robs two others who posted Erotic Services ads.	In May, under pressure from law enforcement and the media, Craigslist makes more changes for posting ads in the Erotic Services category.

2007

On October 25, a young woman is murdered after responding to a Craigslist ad for a nanny.

2008

Working with law enforcement agencies, Craigslist puts in place strict requirements for posting Erotic Services ads.

2008

In April and May, eBay and Craigslist file lawsuits against one another over control of Craigslist.

2009

In June, Newmark launches All For Good, a Web site designed to connect people with projects and activities.

2009

On December 7, eBay and Craigslist go to court.

2010

In September, Craigslist removes the Adult Services category from its US sites. A ruling is made in the case filed in April 2008.

ESSENTIAL FACTS

CREATOR

Craig Newmark, December 5, 1952

DATE LAUNCHED

1995

CHALLENGES

Craigslist has faced conflicts on three fronts. First, people in the newspaper industry have criticized the Web site for taking away much of their business selling classified ads. Second, Craigslist has been under pressure from law enforcement and the media to place restrictions on posting ads that involve people in dangerous or illegal activities. This pressure has come after a number of crimes, including several murders, have been linked to Craigslist ads. Finally, Craigslist has been involved in lawsuits with eBay over control of the Web site.

SUCCESSES

In 1995, as a hobby, Newmark started e-mailing friends and coworkers about arts and technology events in San Francisco, developing the network that would soon become Craigslist. The list quickly grew in popularity and in the amount of information it offered. Continued growth in popularity prompted Newmark to create a Web site in 1995 to replace his e-mail list, which had become a listserv. In 1999, he focused full-time on Craigslist, establishing it as a corporation. Realizing that he was not good at running a company, Newmark hired Jim Buckmaster to take over that role. Newmark continued to work in customer service.

As Craigslist grew, Newmark turned away countless investors and other opportunities to earn huge profits. Instead, he focused on providing a service to the Internet community. By 2009, however, Craigslist was earning $100 million a year and had an estimated value of $1 billion.

IMPACT ON SOCIETY

Millions of people access Craigslist daily in an effort to meet a variety of needs. Users take advantage of the site to look for new homes, new jobs, and new relationships, among other things. The site is a hub for buying and selling new and used items of all sorts, including cars, furniture, clothing, and jewelry. The site has also been used to meet important survival needs. In one instance, a woman posted an ad searching for people to donate a kidney for her ailing husband. Craigslist has changed the way people buy and sell things and exchange ideas and information. Because Craigslist does not charge people to post and view most ads, everyone has access to the Web site. Furthermore, by encouraging people to treat others as they want to be treated, Craigslist has created a culture of trust. Newmark believes strongly in the power of the Internet community to bring about change in society. The charitable organizations with which he is involved use the Internet to connect people and organizations with the resources they need to build strong communities and neighborhoods. Everyday people's use of the Internet is key to furthering citizen journalism, another cause that Newmark supports.

QUOTE

"Give people a break."—*Craigslist's motto*

GLOSSARY

bar mitzvah
The event that marks a 13-year-old boy's becoming an adult in the Jewish community and thus being responsible for his actions.

board of directors
The group of people elected or appointed to oversee the activities of a corporation.

chairperson
The highest-ranking person on a company's or organization's board of directors.

chief executive officer
The person responsible for a company's overall operation and performance.

classified advertisements
Short descriptions of items or services available for sale or rent; the ads are organized by classification or type, such as employment and apartments.

consensual
Describing something that is done with the agreement of everyone involved.

consultant
A professional person hired and paid a fee to provide expert knowledge and advice.

corporation
A type of company formed by one or more owners who are given or sold shares of stock in proportion to the amount of the company they own; similar to an individual, a corporation can borrow money, hire and fire workers, and so on.

evict
　　To remove a tenant from a rental property, usually for not paying the rent.

forensics
　　The science or technology used to establish evidence in a court of law.

network
　　A connected system of people or things.

nonprofit organization
　　A group that works to benefit or support a certain cause or issue; its primary mission, or purpose, is to provide service, not to make profits.

physics
　　The science that studies matter and energy.

post
　　To put information on a Web site.

scamming
　　Tricking or cheating people out of their possessions or money.

scapegoating
　　Blaming or punishing a person for what someone else has done.

spamming
　　Abusing the use of electronic messaging, such as e-mail; usually done by sending out a huge number of messages to people at random, without their request.

synagogue
　　A building for religious worship and instruction in the Jewish faith.

ADDITIONAL RESOURCES

SELECTED BIBLIOGRAPHY

"GovLoop Member of the Week—Craig Newmark, Customer Service Rep and Founder, Craigslist.Org." *Heather Krasna's Public Service Career Blog.* WordPress.com, 8 Feb. 2009. Web. 15 Feb. 2010.

Morris, Richard. "Craig Newmark: Geek of the Week." *Simple-Talk.* Red Gate Software, 2010. Web. 18 Feb. 2010.

Weiss, Phillip. "A Guy Named Craig." *NYMag.com.* New York Media, 2010. Web. 22 Feb. 2010.

Zinko, Carolyn. "A Day in the Life of . . . Craig Newmark." *SFGate. com.* Hearst Communications, 10 Oct. 2004. Web. 18 Jan. 2010.

FURTHER READINGS

Boggs, Bill. *Got What It Takes? Successful People Reveal How They Made It to the Top.* New York: HarperCollins, 2007. Print.

Livingston, Jessica. *Founders at Work: Stories of Startups' Early Days.* Berkeley, CA: Apress, 2007. Print.

Lloyd, Jenna. *Craigslist 4 Everyone.* London: Que, 2009. Print.

Vinjamuri, David. *Accidental Branding: How Ordinary People Build Extraordinary Brands.* Hoboken, NJ: Wiley, 2008. Print.

WEB LINKS

To learn more about Craigslist, visit ABDO Publishing Company online at **www.abdopublishing.com**. Web sites about Craigslist are featured on our Book Links page. These links are routinely monitored and updated to provide the most current information available.

PLACES TO VISIT

Computer History Museum
1401 North Shoreline Boulevard, Mountain View, CA 94043
650-810-1010
www.computerhistory.org
The museum preserves and celebrates the history of computers. It has one of the largest collections of computer artifacts in the world. Visitors can explore the museum themselves or take guided tours.

Smithsonian, National Museum of American History,
Division of Information Technology and Communication
1400 Constitution Avenue NW, Washington, DC 20560
202-633-3877
http://americanhistory.si.edu/about/deptdetailcfm?deptkey=40
This division of the Smithsonian is dedicated to understanding information technologies and their place in US history. Exhibitions are available within the museum and online.

Tech Museum of Innovation
201 South Market Street, San Jose, CA 95113
408-294-8324
www.thetech.org
The museum provides opportunities to experience science and technology. It offers hundreds of exhibits and activities, including some online.

SOURCE NOTES

CHAPTER 1. A UNIQUE COMPANY FOUNDER

1. "Media Interviews—Craig Newmark: Craigslist Isn't a Media Menace." *IWantMedia.com.* I Want Media, 20 Apr. 2007. Web. 15 Feb. 2010.

2. Ira Steiner. "Craigslist Founder Newmark Talks about Customer Service." *AuctionBytes.* Steiner Associates, 2010. Web. 10 Mar. 2010.

3. *Zondervan NIV Study Bible.* Fully rev. ed. Kenneth L. Barker, gen. ed. Grand Rapids, MI: Zondervan, 2002. Print.

4. Carolyn Zinko. "A Day in the Life of . . . Craig Newmark." *SFGate.com.* Hearst Communications, 2010. Web. 18 Jan. 2010.

5. Lidija Davis. "Craig Newmark's Keynote Address Unlock the Secrets to Building a Community." *ReadWriteWeb.com.* ReadWriteWeb, 10 Feb. 2009. Web. 15 Feb. 2010.

6. Greg Sandoval. "Craigslist's Craig Newmark--no more Mr. Nice Guy?" *CNET News.* CBS Interactive, 10 Oct. 2004. Web. 25 Sept. 2010.

7. Bradley Campbell and Matt Snyders. "Craig Newmark Speaks at Victim's Memorial in Wake of Craigslist Killings." *SFWeekly.com.* Village Voice Media, 5 May 2009. Web. 5 Feb. 2010.

8. Ibid.

9. Ibid.

10. "GovLoop Member of the Week—Craig Newmark, Customer Service Rep and Founder, Craigslist.Org." *GovLoop.com.* GovLoop, 8 Feb. 2009. Web. 15 Feb. 2010.

CHAPTER 2. LIFE BEFORE CRAIGSLIST

1. Leslie Bunder. "Craig Newmark Interview." *Something Jewish Online.* JMT Ventures, 12 Nov. 2005. Web. 18 Feb. 2010.

2. Evan Carmichael. "'I Lived the Dilbert Life': The Early Years of Craigslist Founder Craig Newmark." *EvanCarmichael.com.* N.p., n.d. Web. 24 Feb. 2010.

3. Craig Newmark. "Speaking Frankly at GovLoop.com." *CNewmark.com.* Craig Newmark, 8 Feb. 2009. Web. 18 Feb. 2010.

4. Paul Harris. "The nerd who became a crusader." *The Observer.* 19 Feb. 2006. Guardian News and Media, 2010. Web. 25 Sept. 2010.

5. Phillip Weiss. "A Guy Named Craig." *NYMag.com.* New York Media, 8 Jan. 2006. Web. 22 Feb. 2010.

6. Ibid.

CHAPTER 3. STARTING CRAIGSLIST

1. Evan Carmichael. "'I Lived the Dilbert Life': The Early Years of Craigslist Founder Craig Newmark." *EvanCarmichael.com.* N.p., n.d. Web. 24 Feb. 2010.

2. "Craigslist—On the Record: Craig Newmark." *SF Gate.* Hearst Communications, 15 Aug. 2004. Web. 4 Mar. 2010.

3. "Craigslist—On the Record: Craig Newmark." *SF Gate*. Hearst Communications, 15 Aug. 2004. Web. 4 Mar. 2010.

4. Todd R. Weiss. "Q&A: Craig Newmark, of 'Craigslist' Fame, Looks Back—and Ahead." *Computerworld.com*. Computerworld, 24 Dec. 2007. Web. 18 Jan. 2010.

5. Phillip Weiss. "A Guy Named Craig." *NYMag.com*. New York Media, 8 Jan. 2006. Web. 22 Feb. 2010

6. Amy Zipkin. "Not Easily Classified." *NYTimes.com*. New York Times Company, 26 Mar. 2006. Web. 3 Mar. 2010.

7. Todd R. Weiss. "Q&A: Craig Newmark, of 'Craigslist' Fame, Looks Back—and Ahead." *Computerworld.com*. Computerworld, 24 Dec. 2007. Web. 18 Jan. 2010.

8. Brier Dudley. "Craig of Craigslist Talks about Spam, Online Threats, and Feuding Pet Lovers." *Seattle Times Online*. Seattle Times Company, 4 June 2008. Web. 4 Mar. 2010.

CHAPTER 4. AMAZING SUCCESS

1. Todd R. Weiss. "Q&A: Craig Newmark, of 'Craigslist' Fame, Looks Back—and Ahead." *Computerworld.com*. Computerworld, 24 Dec. 2007. Web. 18 Jan. 2010.

2. Stephanie Smith. "Success Stories: Craigslist's Craig Newmark." *SuccessMagazine.com*. Success Magazine, 2010. Web. 3 March 2010.

3. Josh McHugh. "Mr. Craigslist, Master of the Nerdiverse." *Wired.com*. Conde Nast Digital, Sept. 2004. Web. 2 Mar. 2010.

4. Ibid.

5. Ian Katz. "Craigslist, Craig Newmark, and Jim Buckmaster." *Guardian Online*. Guardian News and Media Limited, 4 Nov. 2006. Web. 4 March 2010.

6. Lidija Davis. "Craig Newmark's Keynote Address Unlock the Secrets to Building a Community." *ReadWriteWeb.com*. ReadWriteWeb, 10 Feb. 2009. Web.15 Feb. 2010.

7. "Creating the World's Most Popular List: Craigslist is Born" *EvanCarmichael.com*. N.p., 26 Aug. 2005. Web. 25 Sept. 2010.

8. Josh McHugh. "Mr. Craigslist, Master of the Nerdiverse." *Wired.com*. Conde Nast Digital, Sept. 2004. Web. 2 Mar. 2010.

9. Richard Morris. "Craig Newmark: Geek of the Week." *Simple-Talk.com*. 15 June 2009. Red Gate Software, 2010. Web. 18 Feb. 2010.

CHAPTER 5. PROVIDING CUSTOMER SERVICE

1. Richard Morris. "Craig Newmark: Geek of the Week." *Simple-Talk.com*. Red Gate Software, 15 June 2009. Web. 18 Feb. 2010.

2. "about > help > spam." *Craigslist*. Craigslist, 15 Sept. 2008. Web.18 Jan. 2010.

3. Ibid.

4. Phillip Weiss. "A Guy Named Craig." *NYMag.com*. New York Media, 8 Jan. 2006. Web. 22 Feb. 2010.

SOURCE NOTES CONTINUED

5. Aleksandra Todorova. "A Craigslist Scam You Might Fall For." *SmartMoney.com*. Dow Jones & Company, 10 Aug. 2005. Web. 18 Jan. 2010.

6. Phillip Weiss. "A Guy Named Craig." *NYMag.com*. New York Media, 8 Jan. 2006. Web. 22 Feb. 2010.

CHAPTER 6. DEALING WITH CRIME

1. WGBH Educational Foundation. "Interviews: Craig Newmark." *Frontline*. 3 Nov. 2006. WBGH Educational Foundation, 2010. Web. 2 March 2010.

2. Kristen Mack. "Craigslist robberies: Chicago police arrest 3." *Chicago Tribune*. Tribune Newspaper, 21 Nov. 2009. Web. 25 Sept. 2010.

3. William Yardley. "Online Invitation to 'Help Yourself' Surprises the Stuff's Owner." *NYTimes.com*. New York Times Company, 18 May 2007. Web. 6 Mar. 2010.

4. Jeremy Abelson. "Embrace for Impact: My Conversation with Craig Newmark on the 'Craigslist Killer.'" *The Huffington Post*. HuffingtonPost.com. 28 Apr. 2009. Web. 6 Mar. 2010.

5. "Seven Days of Rage: The Craigslist Killer." *48Hours*. CBS, 19 Sept. 2009. Web. 2 Mar. 2010.

6. Bradley Campbell and Matt Snyders. "Craig Newmark Speaks at Victim's Memorial in Wake of Craigslist Killings." *SFWeekly.com*. Village Voice Media, 5 May 2009. Web. 5 Feb. 2010.

7. Martin Bashir, Arash Ghadisha, and Christina Caron. "Exclusive: Craigslist Founder Doesn't Plan to Change Web Site." *Nightline*. ABC News Internet Ventures, 24 Apr. 2009. Web. 8 Mar. 2010.

8. Jackson West. "Craig Newmark Doesn't Feel Guilty about Craigslist Criminals." *NBCBayArea.com*. NBC Universal, 22 Oct. 2009. Web. 5 Mar. 2010.

CHAPTER 7. FACING THE COMPETITION

1. Phillip Weiss. "A Guy Named Craig." *NYMag.com*. New York Media, 8 Jan. 2006. Web. 22 Feb. 2010.

2. Paul Harris. "The nerd who became a crusader." *The Observer*. Guardian News and Media, 19 Feb. 2006. Web. 25 Sept. 2010.

3. Jackson West. "Craig Newmark Doesn't Feel Guilty about Craigslist Criminals." *NBCBayArea.com*. NBC Universal, 22 Oct. 2009. Web. 5 Mar. 2010.

4. Phillip Weiss. "A Guy Named Craig." *NYMag.com*. 8 Jan. 2006. New York Media, 2010. Web. 22 Feb. 2010

5. "Media Interviews: In Their Own Words—Craig Newmark: Craigslist Isn't a Media Menace." *IWantMedia.com*. I Want Media, 2 Apr. 2007. Web. 8 Mar. 2010.

6. "Craigslist—On the Record: Craig Newmark." *SFGate.com*. Hearst Communications, 15 Aug. 2004. Web. 4 Mar. 2010.

7. Anita Hamilton. "Taking Aim at Craigslist." *Time.com*. Time Inc., 18 June 2008. Web. 4 Mar. 2010.

8. "Complaint Department: Archive for the 'Legal' Category." *Craigslist.org*. Craigslist, 30 Apr. 2008. Web. 10 Jan. 2010.

CHAPTER 8. SERVING THE COMMUNITY

1. Adam Toren. "Profile on Craig Newmark." Young Entrepreneur. *YoungEntrepreneur.com*. 15 Dec. 2009. Web. 15 Feb. 2010.

2. "GovLoop Member of the Week—Craig Newmark, Customer Service Rep and Founder, Craigslist.Org." *WordPress.com*. 8 Feb. 2009. Web. 15 Feb. 2010.

3. "Bio of Craig Newmark: Founder of Craigslist." *The Johnsville News*. N.p., 26 Aug. 2005. 15 Feb. 2010.

4. Craig Newmark. "A Personal Call to Service." The Huffington Post. *HuffingtonPost. com*. 8 July 2009. Web. 16 Jan. 2010.

5. Suzanne Perry. "'Craigslist' for Volunteers to Debut Soon." *Chronicle for Philanthropy*. MSNBC.com, 12 June 2009. Web. 16 Jan. 2010..

6. "About: Our Mission." *CraigslistFoundation.org*. Craigslist Foundation, 2010. Web. 18 Jan. 2010.

7. Gillian Reagan. "Craig Newmark Teams with White House All for Good." *The New York Observer*. N.p., 23 June 2009. Web. 16 Jan. 2010.

8. Craig Newmark. "Why 'Craigslist Founder Joins Veterans Affairs Innovation Search Panel.'" *The Huffington Post*. HuffingtonPost.com, 5 Nov. 2009. Web. 16 Jan. 2010.

9. "GovLoop Member of the Week—Craig Newmark, Customer Service Rep and Founder, Craigslist.Org." *WordPress.com*. 8 Feb. 2009. Web. 15 Feb. 2010.

CHAPTER 9. LIFE TODAY

1. "The Federal 100: Twentieth Anniversary." *1105 Government Information Group*. 1105 Media, 2009. 15 Feb. 2010.

2. "Bio of Craig Newmark: Founder of Craigslist." *The Johnsville News*. N.p., 26 Aug. 2005. Web. 15 Feb. 2010.

3. Carolyn Zinko. "A Day in the Life of . . . Craig Newmark." *SFGate.com*. Hearst Communications, 10 Oct. 2004. Web. 18 Jan. 2010.

4. Ibid.

5. Newmark. Blog. 10 Feb. 2010.

6. "Media Interviews—Craig Newmark: Craigslist Isn't a Media Menace." *IWantMedia. com*. I Want Media, 20 Apr. 2007. Web. 15 Feb. 2010.

7. Richard Morris. "Craig Newmark: Geek of the Week." *Simple-Talk.com*. 15 June 2009. Red Gate Software, 2010. Web. 18 Feb. 2010.

INDEX

ABOUT THE AUTHOR

Susan M. Freese has developed and produced educational materials for students at many levels. She has also taught college-level literature, writing, and communications courses. Susan's interest in music and the arts has involved her in writing promotional and grant materials for several nonprofit organizations. She is also the current president of Minnesota Bookbuilders, a group of professionals who work in various facets of producing books. Susan lives in Minneapolis, Minnesota.

PHOTO CREDITS